P9-BBQ-395

ADVERTISING ART
IN THE
ART DECO STYLE

SELECTED BY THEODORE MENTEN

DOVER PUBLICATIONS, INC.
NEW YORK

Advertising Art in the Art Deco Style, first published by Dover Publications, Inc., in 1975, is a new
selection of illustrations from the sources listed in
the Publisher's Note.

International Standard Book Number: 0-486-23164-X
Library of Congress Catalog Card Number: 74-27703

Manufactured in the United States of America
Dover Publications, Inc.
180 Varick Street
New York, N.Y. 10014

PUBLISHER'S NOTE

During the Art Deco period, the 1920s & 30s, advertising art came into its own as never before in history. The new freedom that allowed outstanding artists to enrich the quality of all useful objects (previously often undervalued as "applied art") was particularly evident in commercial graphics throughout America & Europe.

The present volume contains 363 authentic Art Deco ads, posters, trademarks & other advertising art reproduced directly from original magazines & books published between 1924 & 1940. All sorts of clients are represented, from consumer products to heavy industry, with an emphasis on automobiles & fashions, great specialties of the period. But there is also advertising for airlines, cosmetics, cigarettes, beverages, department stores, printers, art shows, commercial art studios & much more.

One hundred eight artists & studios, from nine different countries, are represented. Nearly all were at the pinnacle of their profession, though some are less well remembered today. Among the unforgotten giants whose work is included are Cassandre, Julius Klinger, Jean Carlu, Walter Teague & Georges Lepape. The Index of Artists at the end of the volume will enable you to locate the work of each contributor.

Every important Art Deco style is shown—the hard-line geometric, the swirling "soft" Art Deco, typography & typographic designs, & the hundreds of individual variations. The 22 items illustrated in full color exemplify the vital & ingenious chromatic sensibilities of the period.

The sources of the illustrations are indicated in the captions by abbreviations, which are to be understood as follows:

ABA — *Advertising and British Art*, by Walter Shaw Sparrow, published by John Lane The Bodley Head, London, 1924.

AMG — *Arts et Métiers Graphiques* (bimonthly magazine), Paris (issues identified in captions by issue number plus month/year date; e.g. "AMG 22, 3/31" = No. 22, March 1931 issue).

DF — Untitled and undated booklet bearing the notice "L'imprimerie Draeger Frères qui s'est assuré la collaboration de A. M. Cassandre a réuni pour vous dans cet album quelques-unes de ses affiches," published by Draeger Frères, Montrouge, France.

GA — *GA; A Presentation of the Diversified Art and Engraving Services Offered by the Graphic Arts Co., Hartford, Connecticut*, 1929.

GG — *Gebrauchsgraphik* (monthly magazine), Berlin (issues identified in captions by month/year date only; e.g., "GG 2/30" = February 1930 issue, which would correspond to Vol. VII, No. 2, publication having commenced in 1924).

JSDS — *Jahrbuch der Schriftgiesserei . . . D. Stempel*, Frankfurt A. M. (only Vol. II, New Year's 1930, has been used).

L — *Life* magazine, New York, issue of August 19, 1926.

MP — *Modern Publicity: 1939-40*, edited by F. A. Mercer & W. Gaunt, published by The Studio, London.

OA — *Outdoor Advertising—the Modern Marketing Force*, published by Outdoor Advertising Association of America, 1928.

PA — *The Penrose Annual; A Review of the Graphic Arts*, published by Lund Humphries & Co., London (only Vol. XXXIX, 1937, has been used).

PP — *Posters & Publicity . . . "Commercial Art" Annual*, published by The Studio, London (only the 1927 volume has been used).

WV — *Westvaco Inspirations for Printers*, published by West Virginia Pulp and Paper Company (identified in captions by issue number).

1: Oswald Voh, for a steamship line (GG 7/37).

2: Tom Purvis, for a London clothier (PP).

3: Tom Purvis (GG 4/30).

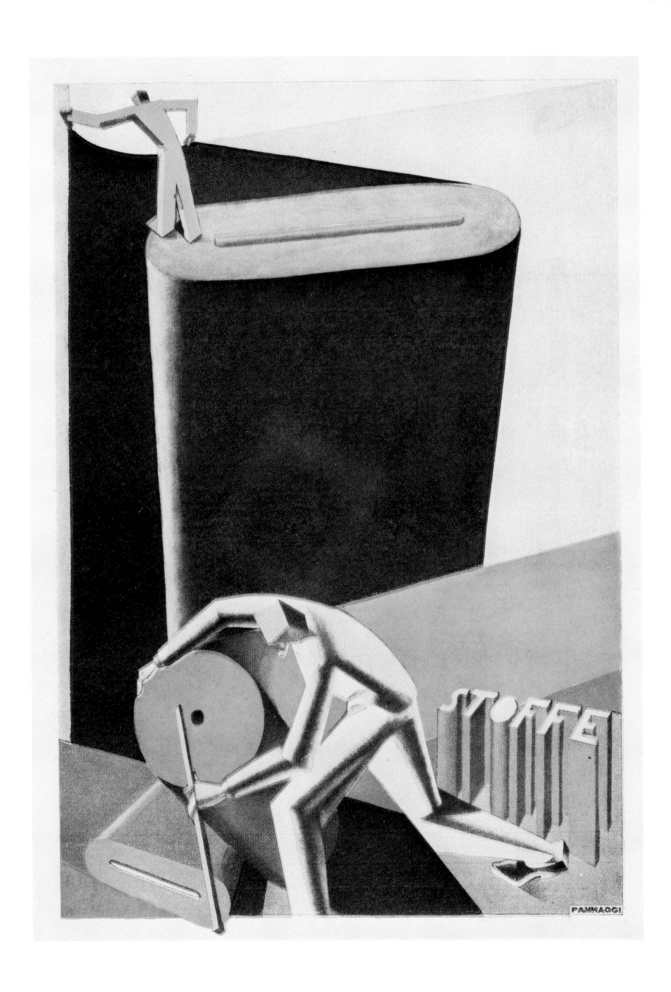

4: Ivo Pannaggi, sketch for a textile poster (GG 5/28).

5: Niklaus Stöcklin, for a consumers' cooperative (GG 3/27).

Wir denken für Sie!

ATELIER SENGER BERLIN W30 ROSENHEIMERSTR.11

Wir zeichnen für Sie

wirksame Inserate, Prospekte, Plakate, Schutzmarken

Werbeberatung auf Grund zwanzigjähriger Erfahrung

6: For a commercial art studio (GG 5/29).

7: For a printer (GG 5/29).

8: Heinz Reichenfelser, for a Danube steamship line (GG 9/37).

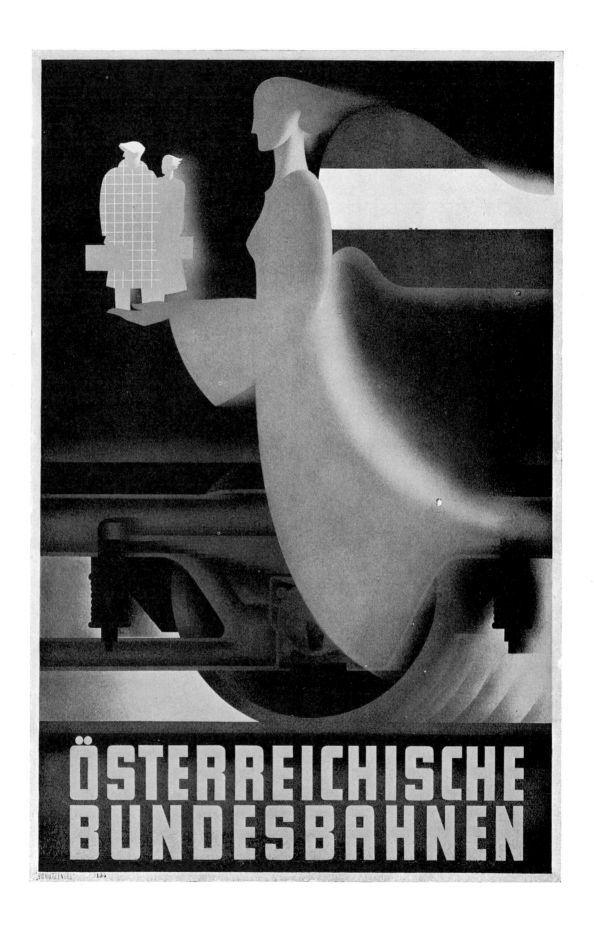

9: Heinz Reichenfelser, for Austrian National Railways (GG 9/37).

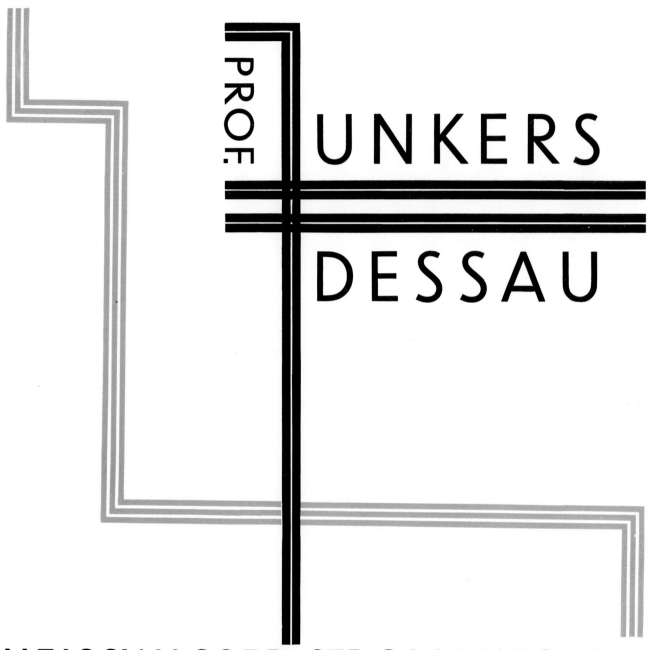

PROF. **JUNKERS** **DESSAU**

HEISSWASSER-STROMAUTOMAT

10: Herbert Thannhaeuser, page from a printer's type brochure
(GG 1/29).

11: Herbert Thannhaeuser, page from a printer's type brochure
(GG 1/29).

12: Alfred Schaefer, for a manufacturer of motors & tools (GG 1/30). 13: Otto Arpke (7/29). 14: Hans Schlier, for household appliances (GG 1/30).

15

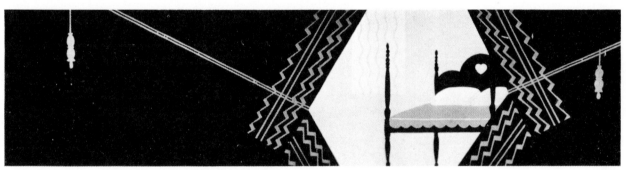

16

17

15–17: J. Asanger (GG 1/29).

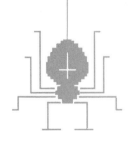

Mein typographisches Selbstbildnis erhebt nicht den Anspruch auf „sprechende Ähnlichkeit"; es hat jedoch eine charakteristische Seite, die ich der Schriftguss A.-G. widme: Aus dankbarer Anerkennung! Weil sie den Mut hatte, die Thannhaeuser-Schriften in ihrem ganzen Umfang herauszugeben. Es darf so genannt sein: Mut!

Eine neue Schrift zeichnen – das ist Sache der Überzeugung und des Glaubens, oft ein Nichtanderskönnen. Eine neue Schrift als Type herausbringen – in einer Zeit, die nur genormten Geschmack kennt und das ganze Glück genießt, nach bewährten Rezepten schöpferisch und patentiert modern zu sein – ist mehr als eine kaufmännische Planung.

Es sei mit ehernen Lettern gesetzt und gedruckt, daß es überall in der Welt Freunde der Freiheit gibt, die eine persönliche Form lieben. Und es sei gesagt, daß neben der rein sachlichen, der objektiven auch die subjektive Form bestehen und ihre eigene Sprache reden wird, wie die Stimmen und Sprachen der Menschen.

THANNHAEUSER

18: Herbert Thannhaeuser, page from a printer's type book (GG 9/35).

19: Heinemann, for an art printer (PP).

GEBR. HARTMANN, HALLE-AMMENDORF
DRUCKFARBENFABRIKEN

Concentrische Kreise

Bathychrom–Braun 31796

20: For a printing ink manufacturer (GG 12/29).

21: Studio Deberny Peignot (AMG 29, 5/32).

22: Type specimen (cigar packaging) (JSDS).

SIE STEIGERN
IHREN UMSATZ
DURCH LICHT-
REKLAME MIT

AGELINDUS

NEON-LEUCHTRÖHREN

AKTIENGESELLSCHAFT
FUER ELEKTRIZITAETS-
INDUSTRIE·BERLIN·W

23: Type specimen (neon lights ad) (JSDS).

24: Friedrich Binder, for an agricultural show (GG 5/25).

25: Heinz Reichenfelser, for a consumers' cooperative exhibition
(GG 9/37).

R · L · LEONARD
IOG CENTRAL PARK WEST
TRAFALGAR 8980
NEW YORK CITY

26: R. L. Leonard (GG 11/26).

27: Jean Carlu, for a performer (GG 12/29).

CREATORS OF THE MODE

The Place de la Concorde, Paris

To the style-conscious woman, the New HUPMOBILE Century car flashes its message of smartness and modernity as swiftly and surely as does the latest gown by the Paris Grande Couture. But to the man who knows HUPMOBILE, there is more than beauty in these New Century cars. In their mechanical trustworthiness he sees them as the same old, game old HUPMOBILES. As rugged as they are regal. As responsive as they are smart. As elegant in their road-manners as they are in their looks. Her car for its dash; his car for its deeds! It is this harmony of approval from both sides of the family that has given these New HUPMOBILE Century cars a sales impetus almost startling, even in the fast-moving motor car industry. The New Century Six, $1345 to $1645; the New Century Eight, $1825 to $2625. All prices f. o. b. factory. Equipment, other than standard, extra.

THE NEW HUPMOBILE
CENTURY SIX & EIGHT

28

CREATORS OF THE MODE

Success is always interesting. And when a long-established business, after 20 years of steady and notable progress, suddenly bounds ahead to an increase of 60% over the previous year, the facts are worth telling and worth reading. To the motor-posted male mind, there never has been any question about HUPMOBILE mechanical quality. For 20 years men have used the word "HUPMOBILE" as a synonym for never-failing motor car integrity. But with the advent of the New Century cars, HUPMOBILE acquired a new recognition. A nation-wide acceptance as the mentor of the motor car mode. Surpassing the richest HUPMOBILE traditions for mechanical excellence, the New Century cars . . . both the Six and the Eight . . . expressed a new and finer art in motor car smartness and beauty. So, today, in the typical American family, he and she are agreed. His car of matchless deed is her car of unrivaled dash. For the HUPMOBILE has been made to look as good as it is! The CENTURY SIX . . . $1345 to $1645. The CENTURY EIGHT . . . $1825 to $2625. Standard and custom. All prices f. o. b. factory. Equipment, other than Standard, extra.

THE NEW HUPMOBILE
CENTURY SIX & EIGHT

29

CREATORS OF THE MODE

EVENING ENSEMBLE BY JENNY
CAR BY . . . HUPMOBILE

Once it was solely a man's car. For he wanted a car that would stand the gaff, as only a HUPMOBILE could, and did. He wanted breathless speed and power; and it gave him more than he ever dared use. He wanted riding comfort, and it rode the roads like a winged chariot on ribbons of air. He wanted freedom from repair bills; and his Hupkeep made his upkeep a genuine pocketbook satisfaction. He wanted durability; and its honesty of materials and its integrity of construction laughed at the years . . . This car still IS a man's car, as sturdy and dauntless as ever, in its mechanism and performance. But today it is HER car, too. For in the New Century Six and the New Century Eight, the HUPMOBILE of deed has become as well, the HUPMOBILE of dash. Inward mechanical perfection has been complemented by distinguished outward beauty . . . So he and she are agreed. Both won to the same car by its mettle and its mode. . What wonder that these New Century cars are enjoying a popular landslide!

THE NEW CENTURY SIX AND EIGHT

You should see the newest Century Cars . . dated today . . with new flair, added modernity, new elegance, in coachcraft and appointments. In both Sixes and Eights there are 49 new body and equipment combinations, standard and custom. The New Century Six $1345 to $1645. The New Century Eight $1825 to $2625. All prices F. O. B. Factory. Equipment, other than standard, extra.

30

28–32: Bernard Boutet de Monvel (GG 11/29).

WHO MADE IT THE MODE ?

EVENING WRAP ... BY MOLYNEUX

CAR ...... BY HUPMOBILE

HE DID and SHE DID , but for different reasons

For years, he had thought of HUPMOBILE as a MAN'S car. Good looking, yet. But its specialty was mileage. Swifter, sweeter mileage. Tireless and endless motor car efficiency.

That was his idea of a HUPMOBILE. A car to shinny up the steepest mountain, or to plough through the meanest morass, without turning a hair. A car with the heart and loins and sinews of a champion. A man's car.

But along came HUPMOBILE with two new cars. The New Century Six and The New Cen-

tury Eight. HUPMOBILE mettle was blended with a new and modern-day mode. Stamina was clothed with Style. The Viking of them all became, as well, the fashion plate of them all.

And his car became HER car, too.

So the other day, when he and she fared forth to choose their 1929 car, she said: "John, let's get a HUPMOBILE!"

And John K. Husband, the rogue, chuckled up his sleeve. For that was the very car he had intended to get, all along.

N. B. . . . This has been going on all over the country. Which accounts for the recent extraordinary unanimity of family opinion on the matter of motor cars. And which also discloses the reason why these New Hupmobile Century cars have won a popular landslide. Prices for the New Century Six, in standard and custom combinations, are $1345 to $1645. The Century Eight, $1825 to $2560 F. O. B., of course, Detroit.

THE NEW Hupmobile
CENTURY SIX AND EIGHT

Handsome is
and Handsome *does!*

Gaze upon a HUPMOBILE Century Six or a Century Eight for the first time. Handsome? Your eyes will not deny that. But HUPMOBILE'S real beauty goes deeper. You must look for it in its motor, in its chassis, in its coachcraft.

For here is the beauty that thrills the engineer. The mathematical beauty of precision and accuracy. Of trustworthy and indefatigable craftsmanship.

You will find it expressed in parts made as finely as watch-works. In bearings, diamond-bored to jewel-like exactness. In pistons fitted by hand to cylinders. In non-chattering valves so snugly contoured that not even the years can loosen their tongues. In metal, shaped and tailored as carefully as a dinner jacket. In materials so staunch and true that no rigors of service can dismay them.

These are the finest "beauty-spots" in HUP-MOBILE. A handsome car, in performance as well as in looks. But if you would know how truly handsome—just drive one!

HUPMOBILE'S new program of expansion has effected sweeping price reductions in the entire Hupmobile line. See your dealer

BEACH COSTUME BY LENIEF

CAR ... BY HUPMOBILE

HUPMOBILE CENTURY SIX ... AND EIGHT

Jane

présentera sa collection à partir du 25 JUILLET.

10 RUE DE LA PAIX
PARIS
COUTURE

33

34

33: Henri Mercier, for a fashion presentation (GG 10/27). **34:** (GA).

35: Calvin Picone, for an art studio (GA).

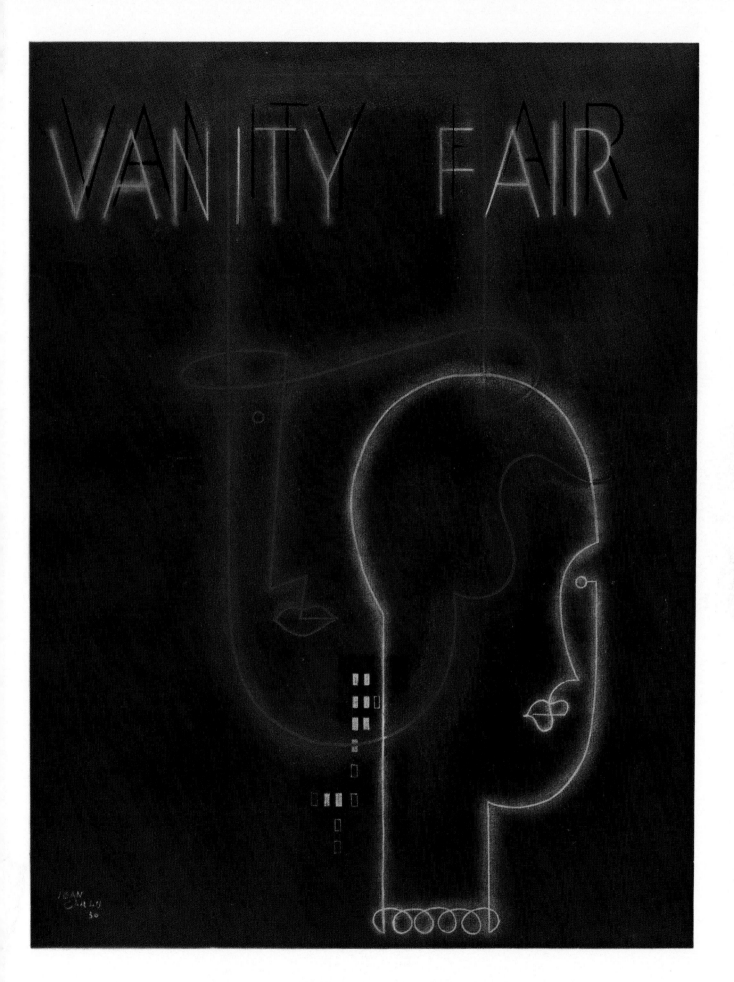

A: Jean Carlu, magazine cover (AMG 24, 7/31).

B

B–F: Léon Bénigni, fashion illustrations & magazine cover (GG 7/30).

C

D

E

F

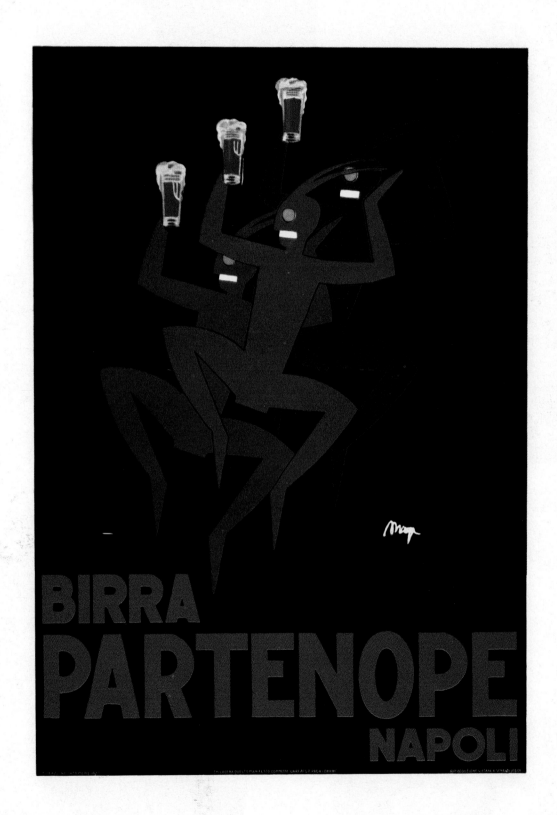

G: Maga (a design studio), for a beer (PP).

H: (WV 65).

I: Jupp Wiertz, for a Zeppelin line (GG 7/37).

DER FRAUEN-KÖNIG

J: J. Fenneker, for a film (GG 6/24).

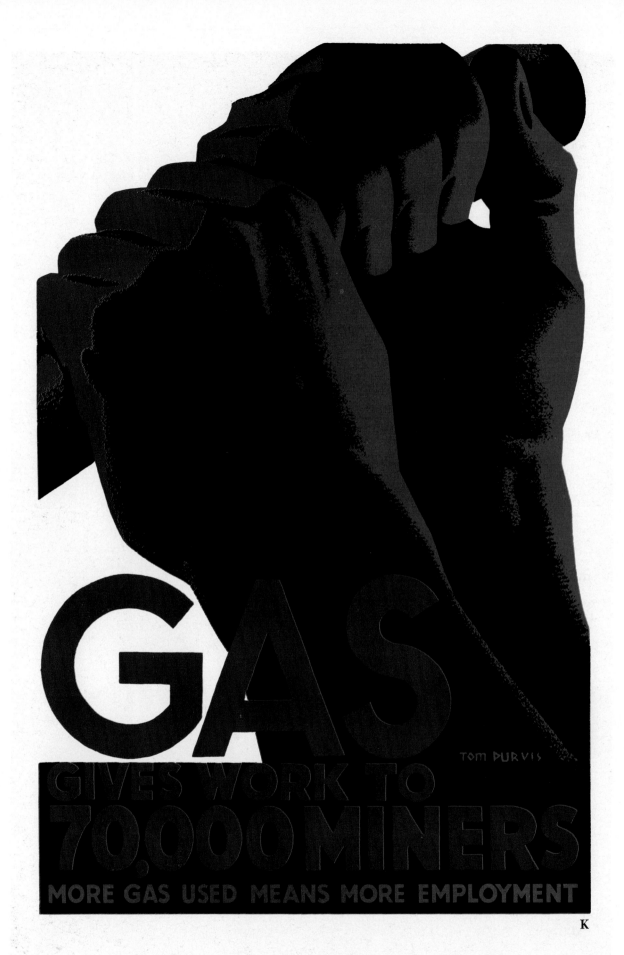

K. Tom Purvis, for a gas company (PA). **L:** Maurice del Mue (OA).
M: A. Armitage (OA). **N:** Walter D. Teague, "Aristocrat in
Motor Cars" (OA).

L

M

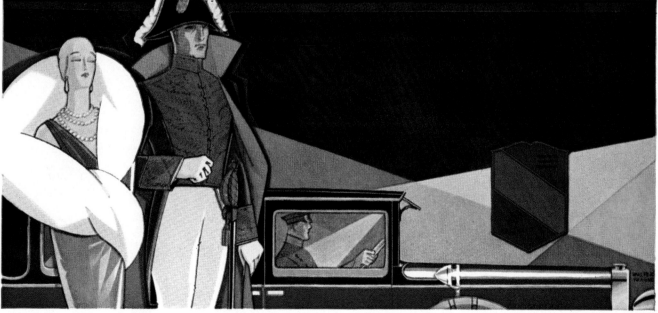

N

O: Walter Riemer, "Eat Fish" (GG 9/30).

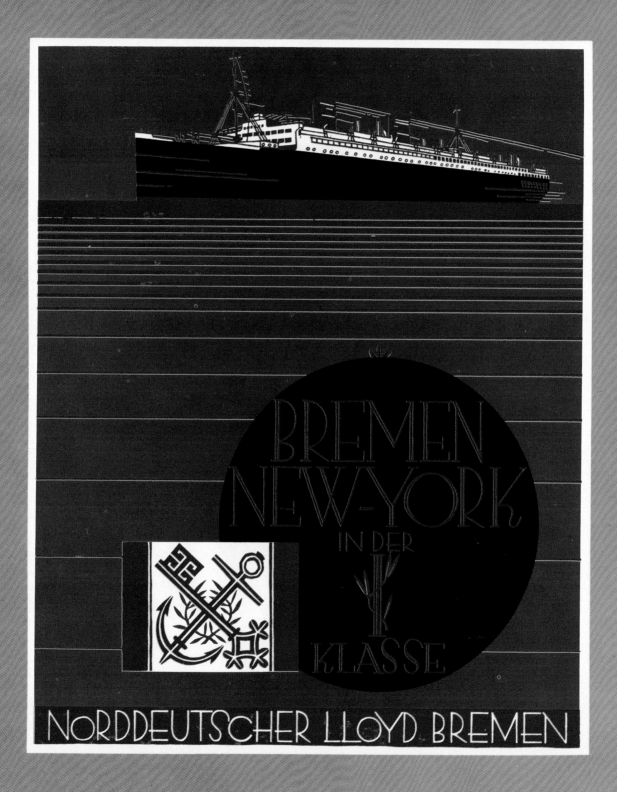

P: For a steamship line (GG 4/28).

Q: Helen Dryden, for a silk company (WV 40). **R:** Eric Fraser,
brochure cover for a gas company (PA).

S: (WV 33).

T: Cassandre, "Greece" (DF).

U

V

U: Otto Arpke, magazine cover (GG 12/30). V: Tom Purvis, for
a London clothier (GG 4/30).

For Christmas
and the
Coming Year
our
Organization
flashes
a cheery thought
in your
direction

The
GRAPHIC ARTS
COMPANY
HARTFORD, CONN.

35

36

37

36 & 37: Cover & spread from a French auto publication (AMG
27, 1/32).

38

39

38: Tadeusz Gronowski, for *Gebrauchsgraphik* magazine (GG 7/28).
39: C. A. Angrave, "Motoring" (ABA).

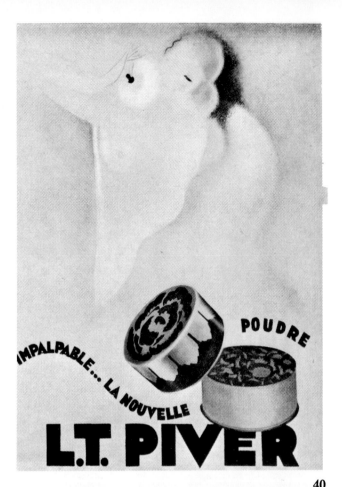

40

41

42

43

40: Charles Loupot, for a cosmetic powder (AMG 24, 7/31).
41–43: Cassandre: for a film daily, a Dutch beer & a Dutch
exhibition (AMG 24, 7/31). **44:** Frederick A. Horn, prospectus
cover (PA).

44

45: For a printer (GG 10/29).

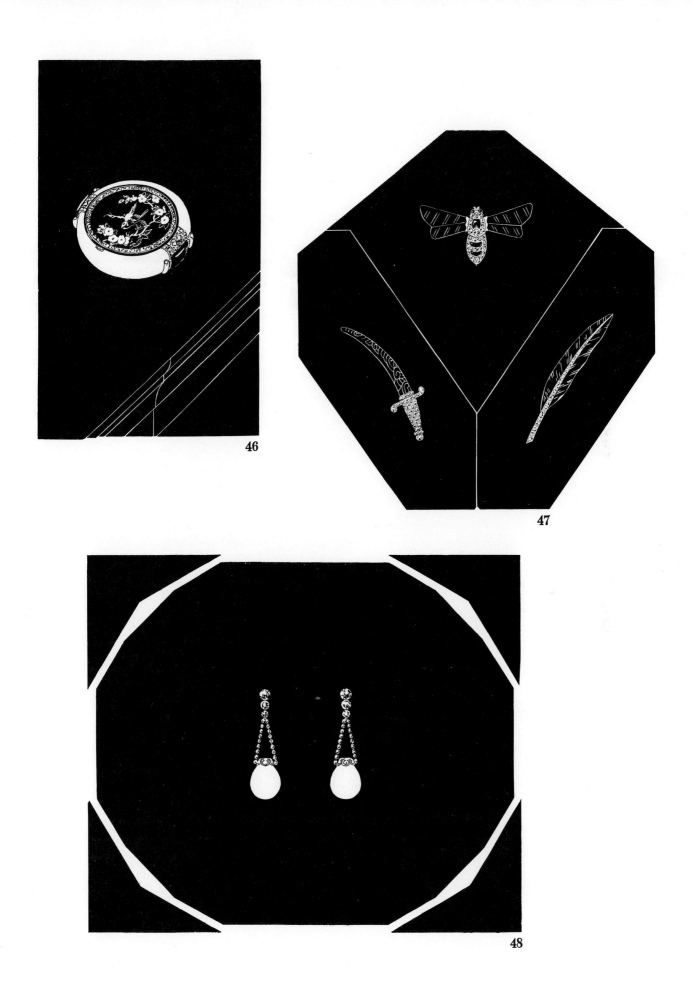

46–48: René Clarke, for a jeweler (GG 10/27).

30

ARTS GRAPHIQUES

ET METIERS

PARIS

49: (AMG 30, 7/32).

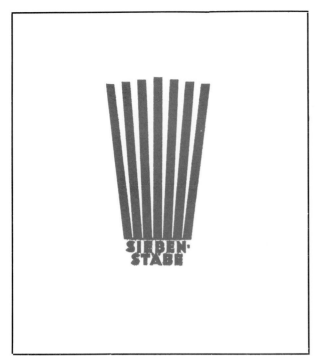

50

51

52

53

50–53: Paul Pfund, for Hamburg civic associations (GG 10/27).

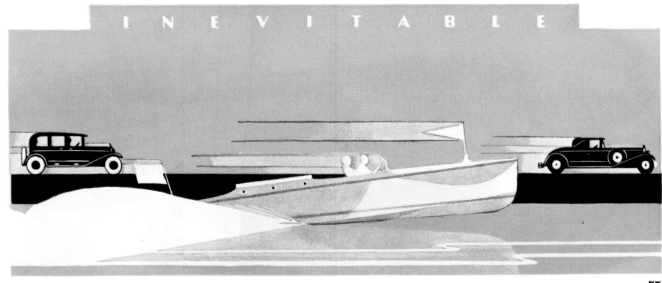

54: Eugen Max Cordier, for an airline (GG 8/31). **55:** (WV 39).

56: Bernd Steiner, for a steamship line (GG 4/28).

57

58

59

57 & 58: Ernst Semmler, for household appliances (GG 1/30 & 11/27). **59:** Karl Schulpig, for ink (GG 11/27). **60:** For an art printer (GG 1/33).

DAS WAHRZEICHEN · DES KUNSTDRUCK's ·

HOCHWERTIGE QUALITÄTS-DRUCKE
Ergebnis jahrzehntelanger Erfahrung, liefern Beweise unseres Könnens. Vielhundert fleis-
siger Menschen schaffende Hände, erstklassige Maschinen moderner Bauart lassen uns
leisten, was man drucktechnisch zu leisten vermag. Wollen Sie werben, werben Sie weise,
wählen Sie sorgsam vom Guten das Beste in Vorbedacht des Erfolges, der Ihnen erwünscht

AKTIENGESELLSCHAFT FÜR KUNSTDRUCK
NIEDERSEDLITZ / SA.

61: Kirnig, for a Munich commerce exhibition (GG 11/27).

62 & 63: Henry Ehlers, for a railroad & a motorcycle (GG 8/31).

INTO THE DEPTHS
IN THE HEIGHT OF FASHION

Women's and Misses' Bathing Apparel—Fifth Floor

SAKS-FIFTH AVENUE
FORTY-NINTH to FIFTIETH STREET, NEW YORK

64–67: Darcy for Saks-Fifth Avenue (GG 4/27).

65

66

67

68

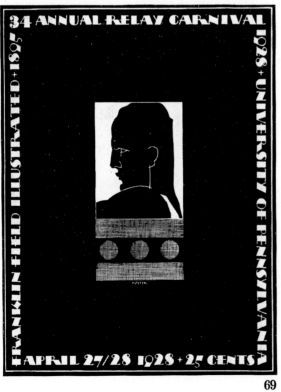

69

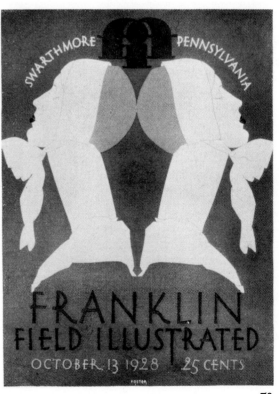

70

68–70: Robert Foster, magazine covers (GG 6/29).

71: Willy Petzold, for a furriers' exhibition (GG 7/29).

72

73

72: Adalbert Roth (GG 8/28). 73: Willy Willrab, for a business-office exhibition (GG 5/25).

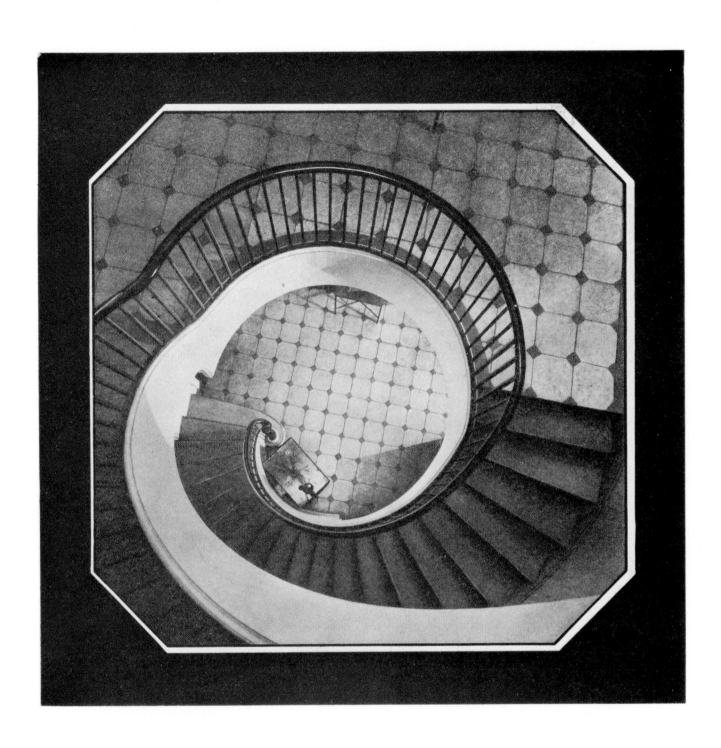

74: (WV 64).

HOUSE & GARDEN

A Condé Nast Publication
March. 1936 ★

ing ening
S Houses
sem Planning

e 35 cents

75

HOSPITAL SERVICE ASS.N
PAYS YOUR
HOSPITAL BILLS
YOU PAY 75c A MONTH

binder

76

HEMMETER   MÜNCHEN

★ GEBIRGS   ENZIAN ★

77

DONAU
ALLGEMEINE VERSICHERUNGS – A. G.
WIEN I., WIPPLINGERSTRASSE 36-38
GRÜNDUNGSJAHR 1867
ALLE VERSICHERUNGSZWEIGE
GEWÄHRLEISTUNGSMITTEL S 100,000 000

78

75–78: Joseph Binder, magazine covers & posters (**77,** "Mountain Gentian," a perfume (?); **78,** for an insurance company) (GG 1/37).

79: Charles Loupot, for a railroad, in connection with a French colonies exhibition (AMG 24, 7/31).

80: R. Blank, for a women's magazine (GG 11/30).

82

83

81–83: Toni Zepf, for a newspaper (in connection with a serialized
sports novel), for a low-alcohol beer & for permanent waves (GG
12/31).

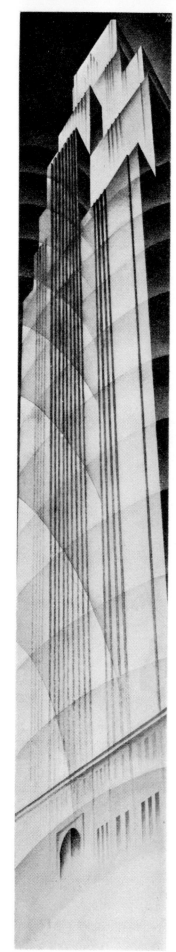

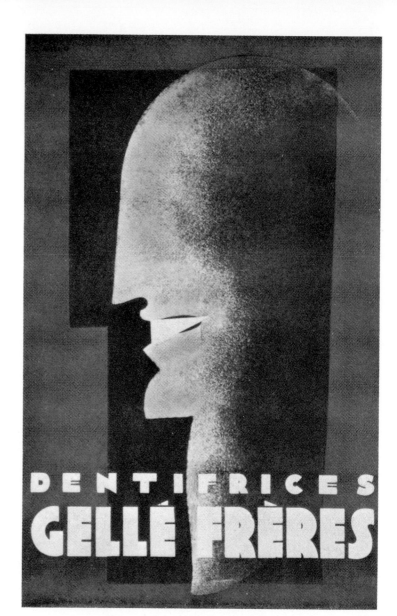

86

85

84

84: (WV 64). 85: Karl Schulpig, for his own services (GG 11/29).

DANS LA TÊTE DE TOUTE FEMME

87

88

FREYTAG & PETERSEN

HANNOVER

METZIG

PAPIERGROSSHANDLUNG

90

89

86–89: Jean Carlu, for toothpaste, a department store, a newspaper
& a magazine (GG 12/29). 90: For a paper dealer (GG 1926).

91

92

91: E. de Coulon, for textiles (GG 5/28). 92: Willy Willrab, for
a cigarette (GG 1926).

93

94

95

93: Joseph Binder, for borax (GG 11/27). 94 & 95: Alfons Plasil,
for ties & hats (GG 11/27).

96

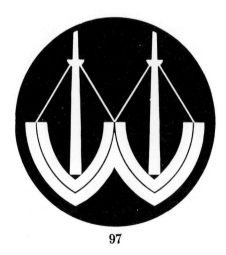

97

96: Hans Ibe, for an optical firm (GG 8/31). **97 & 98:** Fritz Brill
(GG 2/33).

99

98

99: Viktor Slama, for a Soviet exhibition in Vienna (GG 7/29).

BRENNABOR

100

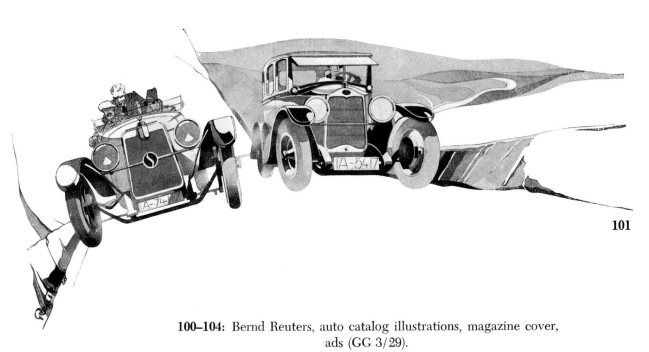

101

100–104: Bernd Reuters, auto catalog illustrations, magazine cover,
ads (GG 3/29).

102

103

104

105

106

107

108

105–108: For a "drink milk" campaign, by Walter Riemer, Dore
Mönkemeyer-Corty, Louis Oppenheim & Willy Wolff, respectively
(GG 3/28).

2 ARBEITEROLYMPIADE
WIEN 1932

109

ABDULLA

110

"CASTELL"
A.W.FABER

111

2 RADIKAL-
DEMO-
KRATEN

verhindert sowohl eine
rote wie eine reaktio-
näre Grossratsmehr-
heit und stimmt Liste

112

109 & 110: Joseph Binder, for a workers' sporting event & a cigarette (AMG 30, 7/32). **111:** For a pencil (GG 9/30). **112:** Robert
Stöcklin, for a political campaign (GG 3/27).

LA LIGNE DE
CYBER

113

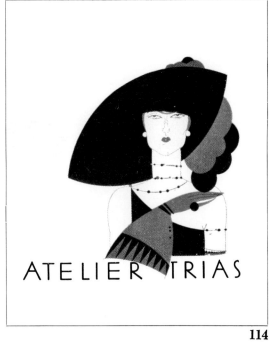

ATELIER TRIAS

114

MONPELAS · PARIS

MALACEÏNE
POUDRE DE RIZ

115

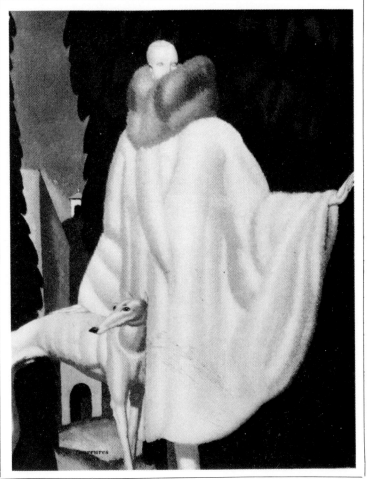

116

QUODLIBET
MASKENBALL
MONTAG 22. FEBR. · KASINO BASEL · HAUPTORCH. 50 MUSIKER
HERREN 20 FR., DAMEN 15 FR. PL. ST. · PRÄMIENSUMME 1200 FR.

117

113: Léon Bénigni, for a couturier (GG 11/30). 114: Atelier Trias
(Rolf Frey), for their own services (GG 1926). 115: Julius Klinger,
for a cosmetic powder (GG 1926). 116: Jean Dupas, for a furrier
(PP). 117: Robert Stöcklin, for a masked ball (GG 3/27).

118

118: Henri Mercier, fashion illustration (GG 10/27). **119–122:**
John Liello (GG 6/27).

women who face
the wind~

119

if you had fifty faces

120

faces ... faces ... faces

121

"the winds are the
warning," says Marie Earle
specialist in faces~

122

123

124

125

123–129: Fromenti, fashion illustrations (**124** is for a hair ornament)
(GG 12/30).

126

127

128

129

130

131

130–133: Fromenti, fashion illustrations & ad for a comb (GG 12/30).

LE PEIGNE
"CRISTAL"
transparent   limpide
EST UNE CRÉATION

132

133

134

135

134–139: Léon Bénigni (GG 1/33 & 7/30).

136

137

138

139

140

141

142

143

140–143: Reynaldo Luza, fashion illustrations (GG 1/33).

144

145

146

144–149: Lotte Wernekink, fashion illustrations (GG 4/29).

147

148

149

150: (WV 37).

VOGUE
SCHNITTMUSTER

Elegante Garderobe hat nicht immer große Mittel
zur Voraussetzung. Mit etwas Geschmack und
einem „Vogue-Schnitt" läßt sich manches aparte
Kleid herstellen, das allen Ansprüchen einer ver-
wöhnten Frau zu genügen imstande ist und dennoch
kaum mehr als den bloßen Stoff kostet. Unter den
zahlreichen „Vogue-Schnittmustern", die Sie neuer-
dings an unserem Schnittmusterlager finden, sind
Modelle, die durch Ruhe und Schönheit der Linie auf-
fallen und andere, die in ihrer jugendlichen Anmut und
Belebtheit dem kapriziösesten Geschmack entsprechen.
Versuchen Sie es mit den „Vogue-Schnitten"!
Schneidern Sie selbst nach „Vogue-Schnitten" oder
geben Sie sie einer Schneiderin zur Ausführung!

LEONHARD TIETZ

151: R. Blank, for clothing patterns (GG 11/30).

Drawn by
L. Bénigni

VELVET AND SILK CREATIONS

COUDURIER
FRUCTUS
DESCHER
LYON PARIS
16-22 E.34 T ST. NEW-YORK

152

153

154

152 & 153: Léon Bénigni (GG 7/30). **154:** (WV 37). **155–157:**
Trias (Rolf Frey), for a night spot (?), perfume & pearls (GG 3/28).

155

156

157

158

159

160

161

158: E. de Coulon, for a publisher (GG 5/28). **159–161:** Georg Lohmann, for a steamship line. **162:** Cassandre, for a steamship line (AMG 25, 7/31).

FRANCE-AMERIQUE DU SUD

PAR
L'ATLANTIQUE
40 000 T.

Cⁱᵉ DE NAVIGATION
SUD-ATLANTIQUE

163: Cassandre, for a cap (GG 6/27).

164: Cassandre, for an atomizer (GG 6/27).

165

165 & 166: Cassandre, for a newspaper & a department store
(AMG 24, 7/31).

166

167

168

169

167–175: Cassandre, for Dubonnet (GG 1/33 & MP).

176

177

178

176: Toni Zepf, for a cigarette (GG 12/31). **177 & 178:** Otto Arpke,
for a printer & for a drink (?) (GG 7/29).

179

180

181

179: Alexander Bortnyik, for a cigarette (GG 11/29). **180 & 181:**
Tadeusz Gronowski, for a tennis tournament & an art show
(GG 7/28).

182: For a commercial art printer (GG 7/28). 183: Rolf Frey,
for shirts (GG 7/29).

MEIN GEBIET ★ DIE INDUSTRIE
PEFFER
FERNRUF: MALER & GRAPHIKER FERNRUF:
STEPHAN STEPHAN
• 8616 • BERLIN • SCHÖNEBERG • MÜHLENSTR.8 • 8616 •

184

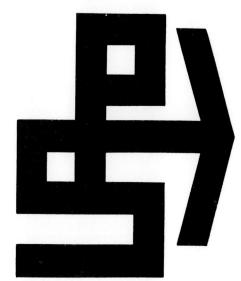

Schutzmarken · Industrie-Entwürfe
Werbedrucksachen

WERBEFACHMANN
PAUL ★ SCHLESINGER
BERLIN W 62, COURBIÈRE STR. 2 ★ LÜTZOW 9936

185

186

184: Franz Peffer, for his own services (GG 1924). 185: Paul
Schlesinger, for his own services (GG 1924). 186: Bergemann,
for a photographic house (GG 1924).

PARIS-BERLIN

187

CITROËN
CITROËN
CITROËN

188

189

DIVERTISSEMENTS TYPOGRAPHIQUES
MAXIMILIEN VOX

190

187, 188 & 190: Typography by the Deberny & Peignot foundry (GG 9/32). 189: Russian typography, "Red Panorama" (GG 3/28).

191

192

196

193

197

200

194

195

198

199

191–200: Rudolf Bossek, for film companies & a toothbrush (GG 12/32).

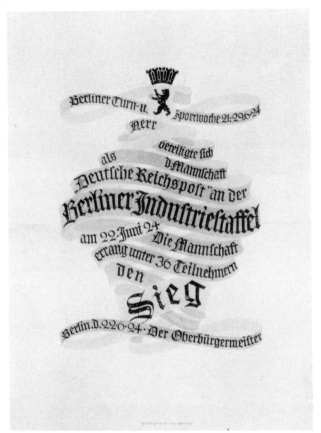

201

202

203

204

205

201–212: Georg Goedecker, typographic designs (201 is a certificate
of sports achievement, 202 is for a costume ball, 204 is a New Year's
greeting, 206 is a coupon for a free portrait by pen or photo, 208
is for a printer, 209 is a greeting card from an art school faculty (?),
211 is a magazine cover (GG 6/29).

BUNTE
LATERNE

FEBRUAR 1929

HERR

WIRD SIE
NACH IHREM WUNSCHE
IN SEINEM

ATELIER

NACH VORHERIGER
ANMELDUNG UND GEGEN
ABGABE
DES ANHANGENDEN
ABSCHNITTES 2

ZEICHNEN

SIE SIND GEGEN ABGABE DES ANHANGENDEN
ABSCHNITTES 3
ZU EINER PHOTOGRAPHISCHEN

GRATISAUFNAHME

WÄHREND DES FESTES BERECHTIGT

DER VORSTAND
DES VEREINS FÜR
DEUTSCHES
KUNSTGEWERBE
BERLIN

206

207

208

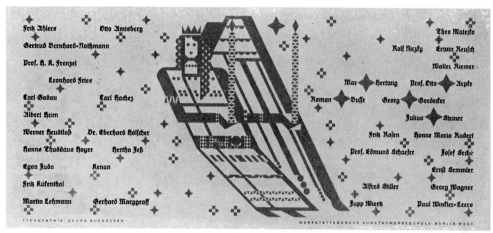

209

210

211

212

213–215: Ernst Aufseeser, a certificate of sports achievement, a
trademark & a typographic design (GG 12/32).

214

215

AT THE SIGN OF

THE FOUR POSTER

216

217

218

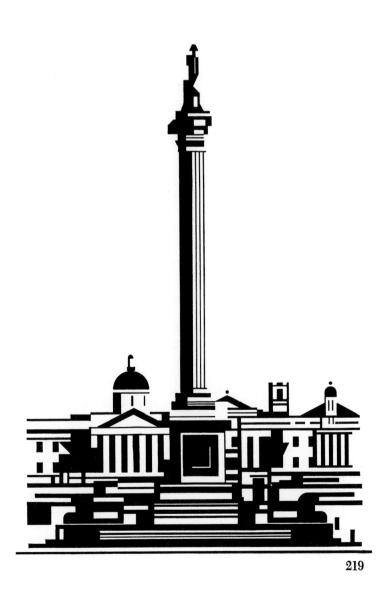

219

216–219: Ernst Aufseeser, an ad & typographic designs (GG 12/32).

BUCHDRUCKEREI

GRUNWALD
& CASIMIR

BERLIN S 14

DRESDENER STRASSE 97

F 1, MORITZPL. 4505, 6018

DIE DRUCKEREI FÜR INDIVIDUELLE MODERNE DRUCKSACHEN

220

220 & 221: Georg Goedecker, typographic ads for a printer & a custom tailor (GG 6/29).

222 & 223: Zero (Hans Schleger) (GG 7/29).

JULIUS RUNGE

SCHNEIDERMEISTER

BERLIN-STEGLITZ
MARIENDORFER STR.50
AMT STEGLITZ 3231

HERRENMODEN

NACH MASS

221

222

223

EIN ASS
in den Karten Ihres
Werbefeldzuges und

**EIN NEUES
INSTRUMENT**
im Orchefter Ihrer gefamten
Reklame wird für Sie die

TYPOGRAPHIE GEORG GOEDECKER
CHARLOTTENBURG 9 · SPANDAUER BERG 9 · WESTEND 6109

224: Georg Goedecker, for his own services (GG 6/29).

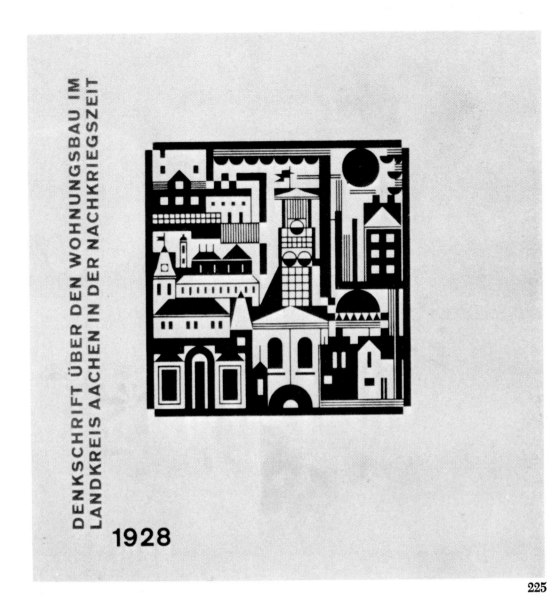

225: Wilhelm Wörner, typographic title page for booklet on housing construction (GG 9/30). **226 & 228:** J. Ehlers, logographs (GG 2/28).
227: W. Kleinschmidt, trademark (GG 2/28).

229–232: Max Körner, trademarks (GG 10/29). **233–235:** Erwin
Reusch, trademarks. (**233** is for air filters) (GG).

236

MOTURBA

237

ADDIATOR

238

HORBACHSTAHL

239

240

241

236–239: Karl Schulpig, trademarks (GG). 240 & 241: E. Charall, trademarks (240 for a petroleum company) (GG).

242

243

242 & 243: Ernst Aufseeser, wall decoration in an exhibition hall
& a logograph (GG 12/32).

244

245

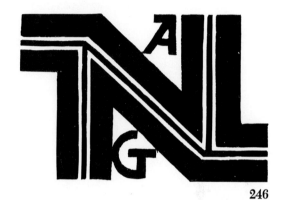

246

247

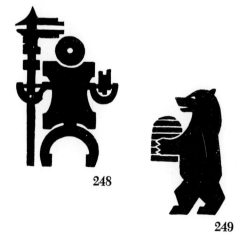

248

249

250

244: Ernst Böhm (GG 1926). **245–247:** Max Körner, trademarks
(**245** is for a mirror factory) & a logograph (GG). **248 & 249:** Trademarks for a measuring instrument manufacturer (GG). **250:** Ernst
Aufseeser, typographic design (GG 12/32).

251: Julius Klinger, for a printer (GG 11/27).

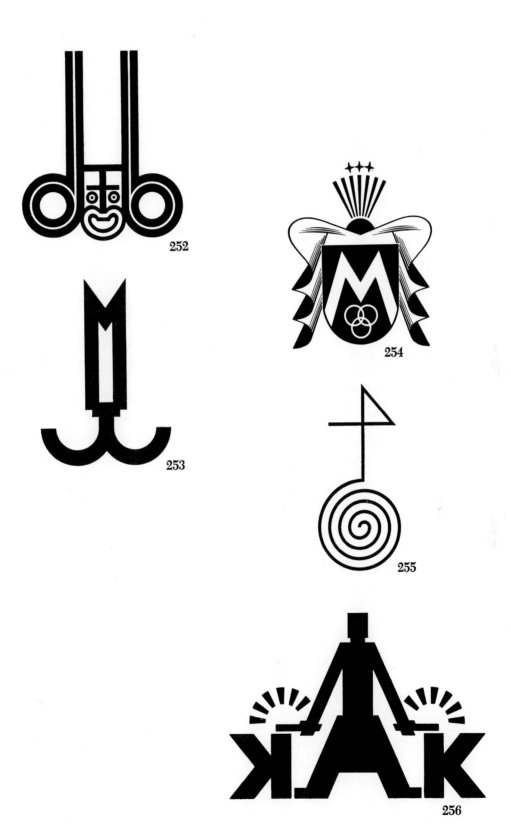

252–256: William Metzig, trademarks (**255** is for a clock) (GG 9/35).

OTTO WOLF BERLIN-STEGLITZ
ALBRECHTSTR.30 · STEGLITZ 9949

257

Ich selbst
mit meinen
Vögeln

METZIG · HANNOVER · CRANACHSTR.

258

Dieses verdammte Gerenne

259

SCHUTZ-
MARKEN
PLAKATE
KATALOGE
PACKUNGEN
ETC.

HUCH
HANNOVER
NELKEN-STR
RUF:
WEST 1806

260

WANDERS/HILDEBRAND
MALER U. GRAPHIKER
B·D·G   V·D·R
HANNOVER / SEILWINDERSTR. 5

261

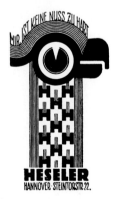

HESELER
HANNOVER · STEINTORSTR. 22.

262

SIGISMUND · FELIX · LEHMANN

LEIPZIG · S3 · LÖSSNIGERSTR 20 · RUF 30291·

263

257: Otto Wolf, for his own services (GG 1/30). 258 & 259: William
Metzig, for his own services & for an alarm clock (GG 1926). 260:
Huch, for his own services (GG 1926). 261: Wanders/Hildebrand,
for their own services (GG 1926). 262: Heseler, for his own services
(GG 1926). 263: Sigismund Felix Lehmann, for his own services
(GG 1/30).

GEBRAUCHSGRAPHIK

JAHRGANG 1

HEFT 6

DER FILM

ARPKE

MONATSSCHRIFT ZUR FÖRDERUNG KÜNSTLERISCHER REKLAME
VERLAG: PHÖNIXDRUCK UND VERLAG G.M.B.H. BERLIN SW 68

264. Otto Arpke, cover of GG 6/24.

Courtesy of Steinway & Sons   Prepared by N. W. Ayer & Son
                    Line engraving

266

267

265

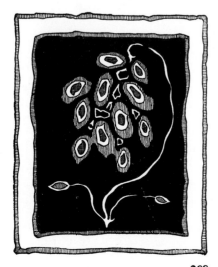

268

265 & 268: (WV 33). **266**: Bobritsky, for a piano firm (WV 33).
267: For a perfume (WV 33).

SMARTNESS THROUGH ASSOCIATION OF IDEAS

269

MODERNISTIC

TREATMENT

OF

ILLUSTRATION

AND COPY

270

269 & 270: (WV 33).

271

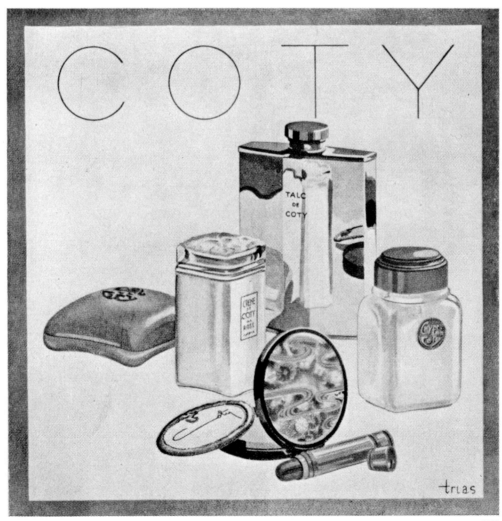

272

271 & 272: Trias (Rolf Frey), for cosmetics (GG 3/28).

273

274

273 & 274: Dore Mönkemeyer-Corty, for tiles & for her own services
(GG 4/27).

275: Cassandre, for an apéritif (PP).

277

276

278

DENT'S GLOVES

279

276: Mela Koehler (PP). **277:** Hemjic (PP). **278:** E. & L. Damour,
for clothing (PP). **279:** Henry Le Monnier, for gloves (PP).

280: For an aluminum company (WV 68).

281

282

284

283

281–283: Walter Riemer, for a league of technical office workers, a pineapple drink & a hair wash (GG 9/30). 284: Dryden (Ernst Deutsch) (GG 7/29).

285

286

287

285 & 286: Léon Bénigni, fashion illustration & magazine cover
(GG 7/30). 287: (WV 68).

289

288

290

288: Georges Lepape (GG 12/29). **289:** Léon Bénigni, fashion illustration (GG 7/30). **290:** Fromenti, for a comb (GG 12/30).

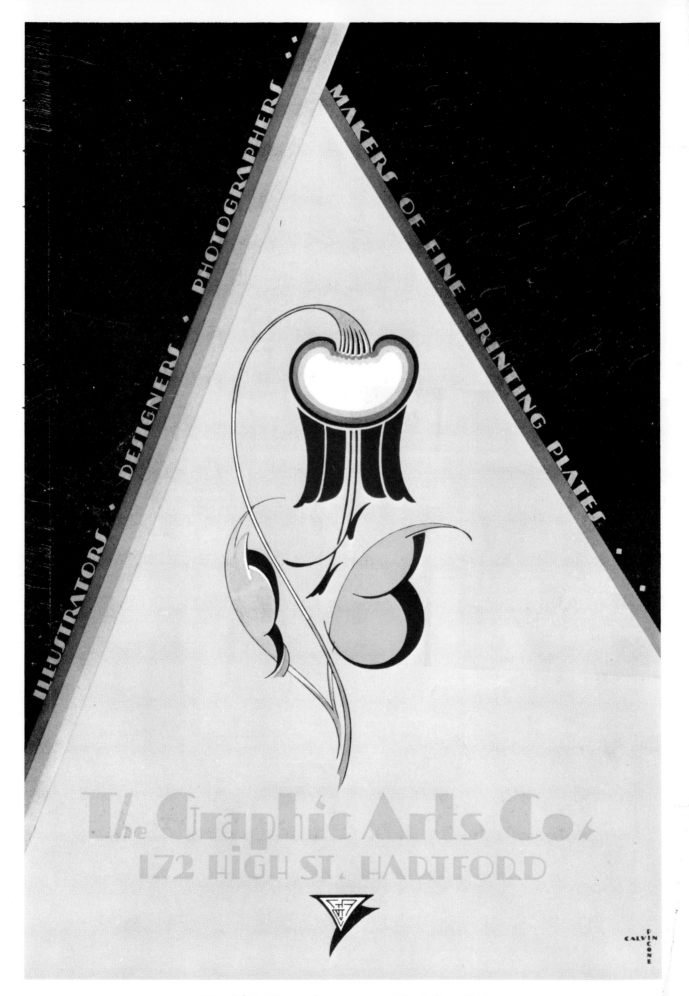

291: Calvin Picone, for a commercial art firm (GA).

292

292–294: Zero (Hans Schleger) (GG 11/26).

295

296

297

295: Joseph Binder, sports ad (GG 1/33). 296 & 297: Ernst Semmler, for a manufacturer of motors & tools (GG 1/30).

298

299

300

298: Joseph Binder, for an exhibition of model homes (GG 1/33).
299: Cassandre, for a drink (GG 1/33). 300: Tadeusz Gronowski,
for a cocoa powder (GG 5/28).

301

302

301 & 302: Walter Riemer, for an interior decoration show & a clothing manufacturer (GG 1/33).

303

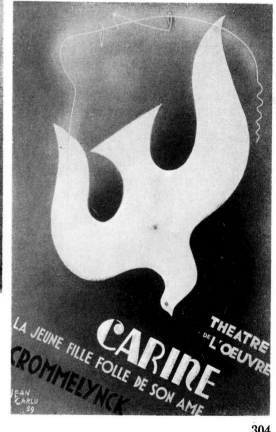

304

303 & 304: Jean Carlu, for Green Shirt organization & a play
(GG 1/33).

Plakat und Warenzeichen

305

306

305: Max Körner, for a canal bond issue (GG 10/29). **306:** Walter
Riemer, magazine cover (GG 9/30).

307

308

307: Toni Zepf, for a railroad (GG 12/31). 308: Ernst Erbe, for
artist's paints (GG 1/30).

309: Atelier Senger, for a travel agency (GG 4/29). 310 & 311:
Hanns Wagula, for a steamship line (GG 11/29).

FLUGZEUG ÜBER DEM
FLUGHAFEN IN TEMPELHOF

312

PIONIER Faltboot und Zelt verschaffen Ihnen gesunde
und billige Ferientage.
Sie kehren nach einer
geruhsamen Wande-
rung auf einsamen Flüs-
sen und Seen mit wirk-
lich gestärkten Nerven
zu Ihrer Arbeit zurück.

Werbeschrift kostenlos von der Pionier Faltboot-Werft Bad Tölz

313

PIONIER
Faltboot und Zelt verschaffen Ihnen
gesunde und billige Erholung. Die
schnittige Form, der leichte Auf-
bau und die Stabilität des Bootes
werden Ihnen immer wieder Freude
machen. Werbeschrift mit genauer
Beschreibung kostenlos durch die
Pionier-Faltboot-Werft, Bad Tölz 24.

314

312: Otto Arpke (GG 12/30). **313 & 314:** Atelier Senger, for
collapsible boats (GG 4/29).

315: Will Hollingsworth (WV 33).

316: Hugh Ferris (WV 37).

317

318

319

320

317–320: Bernd Reuters, for autos (GG 3/29).

321: Bernd Reuters, for an auto (GG 3/29). **322:** Stults (L).

THE NEWEST VOGUE   AMONG FINE CARS

THE MOST BEAUTIFUL   CAR HUPMOBILE HAS
EVER BUILT. NO FINER   PERFORMANCE AT ANY
PRICE. A PERFECTION   OF THE STRAIGHT-EIGHT
THAT GIVES THE WORD   PRESTIGE AN ENTIRELY
NEW MEANING FOR   THOSE WHO NEVER OWN
OR DRIVE ANY BUT THE   FINEST CARS. BEAUTY,
COLOR OPTIONS, LUXURY,   IN SEVEN ENCLOSED AND
OPEN BODIES $1945 TO $2495   F.O.B. DETROIT, PLUS REVENUE TAX

IN THE FINE CAR FIELD, THE TREND   IS UNDOUBTEDLY TOWARD EIGHTS

THE DISTINGUISHED
HUPMOBILE
EIGHT

PIERCE · ARROW · TOWN · CAR

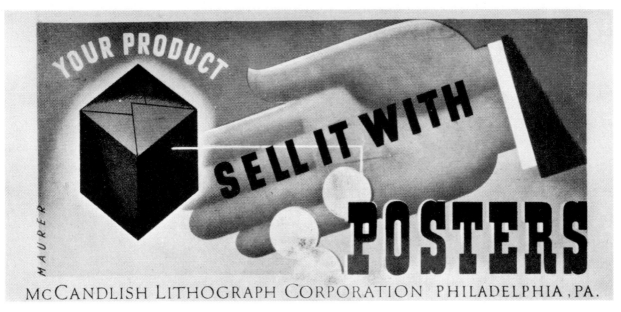

324

325

326

323: (WV 64). 324: Sasha Maurer (MP). 325: John Atherton (MP).
326: Joseph Binder (MP).

327: F. C. Herrick (ABA).

328

329

330

328–330: J. Asanger (OA).

DICKE BOHNEN

ZIGARETTE
UNERREICHT IN GRÖSSE U. QUALITÄT
20₃
ADLER COMPAGNIE ZIGARETTENFABRIK A·G. DRESDEN

331: Walentin Zietara (GG 5/24).

SAYING MUCH
IN LITTLE

332: For a hosiery company (WV 33).

333

334

333: F. C. Herrick (ABA). 334: Walter D. Teague, "Aristocracy in
Motor Cars" (OA).

335

336

335: C. Paine (ABA). **336:** Jon O. Brubaker (OA).

337

337: Robert Cheveux, magazine cover (WV 69). **338–340:** Otto
Arpke, magazine cover, airline poster & illustration (GG 1/33).

338

339

340

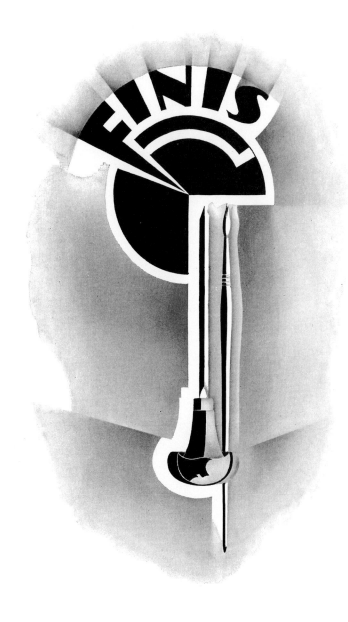

341: (GA).

INDEX OF ARTISTS

The letters refer to the full-color illustrations, the numbers to the black & white illustrations. The nationalities given for the artists sometimes indicate the country of their professional careers rather than of their birth.